John Paul Jones and the Birth of the American Navy

Sarah Crickard

NEW YORK

Published in 2016 by The Rosen Publishing Group, Inc.
29 East 21st Street, New York, NY 10010

Library of Congress Cataloging-in-Publication Data

Crickard, Sarah.
 John Paul Jones and the birth of the American Navy / Sarah Crickard. -- First edition.
    pages cm. -- (Spotlight on American history)
 Includes bibliographical references and index.
 ISBN 978-1-4994-1762-3 (library bound) -- ISBN 978-1-4994-1759-3 (pbk.) -- ISBN 978-1-4994-1757-9
(6-pack)
 1. Jones, John Paul, 1747-1792--Juvenile literature. 2. Admirals--United States--Biography--Juvenile literature.
3. United States. Navy--Biography--Juvenile literature. 4. United States--History--Revolution, 1775-1783--Naval
operations--Juvenile literature. I. Title.
 E207.J7C895 2016
 359.0092--dc23
 [B]
                                        2015014251

Manufactured in the United States of America

CPSIA Compliance Information: Batch #WS15PK: For Further Information contact Rosen Publishing, New York, New York at 1-800-237-9932

CONTENTS

EARLY LIFE IN SCOTLAND

The father of the American navy, John Paul Jones, was born John Paul on July 6, 1747. John Paul was raised in Scotland as the son of a gardener. The future sea captain grew up in sight of the sea. As a boy, he played along the shore and watched ships as they passed along the coast.

Little is known about John's childhood except that he was the fifth of seven children. At an early age,

This photo shows John Paul Jones's town of birth. He was born in the county of Kirkcudbrightshire, on the southwest coast of Scotland.

This 1779 engraving shows the busy port of Liverpool. Young men such as John Paul would come to ports like this to look for work.

he had learned enough mathematics to enable him to learn **navigation.** It was a valuable skill, and few sailors in those times had mastered it.

Scotland in the mid-1700s was poor, but there was opportunity for someone who worked hard to learn a trade. When John reached his 13th birthday, his father **apprenticed** him to the owner of a **merchant** ship.

A BOY GOES TO SEA

During his first voyage, John served as a ship's boy on the ship *Friendship*. The small vessel first stopped at Barbados in the West Indies. It then stopped at Chesapeake Bay, where John got to see his brother William. William had moved from Scotland to Virginia. At the time of John's visit, William was the owner of a tailor shop. William probably told John of the opportunities open to people in the American colonies.

Over the next three years, the *Friendship* sailed many times carrying **provisions** and goods to the West Indies. The sugar, rum, salt, and other products received in exchange were then taken to Chesapeake Bay in Virginia. There they were traded for such items as tobacco and barrels of flour, which were then returned to England. Each trip took most of a year. It was not an easy life, but John Paul liked it. When the owner of the *Friendship* lost his money in 1764, John Paul found himself without a job. In his late teens, he was too old for anyone to take him on as an apprentice but too young to get a good-paying job.

This map of 1774 shows North America and the West Indies. Captain Jones used a map such as this as he sailed in these waters.

BECOMING A CAPTAIN

Down on his luck, John Paul had to take whatever work he could find. He made at least three, and possibly as many as six, voyages in slave-trading vessels. These vessels exchanged British-made goods for people sold as slaves in West Africa. They then carried that cargo of slaves across the Atlantic to the West Indies. John Paul could not long stand what he called the "abominable trade." By 1768, he had saved enough money to leave the evil business and board the ship *John* when it sailed for Scotland from Kingston, Jamaica.

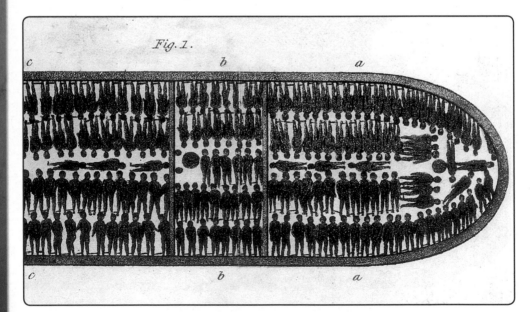

This 18th-century diagram shows the brutal conditions on a slave ship. Slaves were kept below deck, with little room and no fresh air.

The Sugar Mill.

The Sugar works

The Sugar Canes

This engraving shows slaves being forced to work on a sugar plantation. Slaves were often forced to work as many as 18 hours a day.

There was much disease in the West Indies. Yellow fever and malaria **epidemics** killed hundreds of Europeans every year. The captain and first mate of the *John* both died of fevers during the trip to England. John Paul was the only man on board the ship who knew how to navigate. So he became captain. He was 21 years old.

Thankful to John Paul, and knowing that the sailors respected him, the owners asked him to be the permanent captain of the ship. It was a small vessel, but it was a start for the young sailor.

BECOMING JOHN PAUL JONES

Captain Paul received a **salary** for sailing the *John*. He may have also received some of the profits of each voyage. John Paul invested his money wisely with a planter in the West Indies.

Paul ran into some trouble while in Tobago in 1773. He was in Tobago to buy a cargo for transport to Britain. He angered his sailors when he refused to pay them in advance for the trip. When the leader of the **mutinous** sailors rushed at John Paul with a club to hit him on the head, the captain killed the man with his sword. John Paul was afraid that friends of the sailors would influence the court of Tobago to send him to prison. He fled to America. He took the last name "Jones" to hide his identity until the time was better for his return to Tobago.

He arrived in North America at a time when relations between the colonies and Britain were getting worse. In early 1774, the British **Parliament** passed the Coercive Acts to punish Boston for dumping tea in Boston Harbor. This event was known as the Boston Tea Party. The colonists called these acts the Intolerable Acts. The acts made the colonists resist Great Britain.

VOTES and PROCEEDINGS of

the Town of

BOSTON,

JUNE 17, 1774.

AT a legal and very full meeting of the freeholders and other inhabitants of the town of Boston, by adjournment at Faneuil-hall, June 17, 1774.

The Hon. JOHN ADAMS, Esq; Moderator.

UPON a motion made, the town again entered into the confideration of that article in the warrant, Viz. "To confider and determine what meafures are proper to be taken upon the prefent exigency of our public affairs, more efpecially relative to the late edict of aBritifh parliament for blocking up the harbour of Bofton, and annihilating the trade of this town," and after very ferious debates thereon,

VOTED, (With only one diffentient) That the committee of correfpondence be enjoined forthwith to write to all the other colonies, acquainting them that we are not idle, that we are deliberating upon the fteps to be taken on the prefent exigencies of our public affairs; that our brethren the landed intereft of this province, with an unexampled fpirit and unanimity, are entering into a non-confumption agrement; and that we are waiting with anxious expectation for the refult of a continental congrefs, whofe meeting we impatiently defire, in whofe wifdom and firmnefs we can confide, and in whofe determinations we fhall chearfully acquiefce.

Agreable to order, the committee of correfpondence laid before the town fuch letters, as they had received in anfwer to the circular letters, wrote by them to the feveral colonies and alfo the sea port towns in this province fince the reception of the Bofton port bill; and the fame being publicly read,

VOTED, unanimoufly, That our warmeft thanks be tranfmitted to our brethren on the continent, for that humanity, fympathy and affection with which they have been infpired, and which they have expreffed towards this diftreffed town at this important feafon.

VOTED, unanimoufly, That the thanks of this town be, and hereby are, given to the committee of correfpondence, for their faithfulnefs, in the difcharge of their truft, and that they be defired to continue their vigilance and activity in that fervice.

Whereas the Overfeers of the poor in the town of Bofton are a body politic, by law conftituted for the reception and diftribution of all charitable donations for the ufe of the poor of faid town,

VOTED, That all grants and donations to this town and the poor tnereof at this diftreffing feafon, be paid and delivered into the hands of faid Overfeers, and by them appropriated and diftributed in concert with the committee lately appointed by this town for the confideration of ways and means of employing the poor.

VOTED, That the town clerk be directed to publifh the proceedings of this meeting in the feveral news papers.

The meeting was then adjourned to Monday the 27th of June, inftant.

Atteft,

WILLIAM COOPER, Town Clerk.

This document of 1774 reports on a Boston town meeting led by John Adams. In their meeting, the citizens of Boston responded to Britain's Boston Port Act. This law was passed in reaction to the Boston Tea Party to prevent goods from coming into Boston Harbor.

In September, 12 colonies sent delegates to the First Continental Congress in Philadelphia to oppose Parliament. In October, the delegates formed the Continental Association. The association asked Americans to refuse to trade with Britain or use British goods until Parliament repealed the Intolerable Acts and changed British trade and taxation laws.

THE BEGINNING OF THE AMERICAN REVOLUTION

Early in 1775, citizens of Massachusetts began collecting weapons in Concord. The colonists wanted to use the weapons to fight against the British. General Thomas Gage was the commander of the British troops in Boston. Gage was ordered to send a party of soldiers to take the colonists' weapons. On their way to Concord, the British troops were told to stop in Lexington and capture John Hancock and

Thomas Gage was the military governor of Massachusetts in the years 1774 to 1775. Gage had little success against the determined American patriots.

This painting shows the British redcoats advancing against American militiamen at the Battle of Bunker Hill. The British suffered heavy losses during the battle.

Samuel Adams. The British wanted to prevent Hancock and Adams from traveling to Philadelphia to attend the Second Continental Congress.

In both towns, the British regulars fought with colonial minutemen and **militia**. Both sides said the other fired first. This was the "shot heard 'round the world." It was the beginning of the Revolutionary War. On June 17, British soldiers again fought with American militiamen, this time at Breed's Hill. The battle would become known as the Battle of Bunker Hill. News of this event reached Virginia and John Paul Jones.

SAILING AND FIGHTING FOR THE CONTINENTAL NAVY

In September 1775, the 28-year-old Jones made his way to Philadelphia where he offered his services as a captain to the Second Continental Congress. He was given the job of supplying the ships that the congress had bought to form the navy.

He accepted command of the ship *Providence* in May 1776. Jones's first job as captain was to protect merchant

IN CONGRESS.

The DELEGATES of the UNITED STATES of *New Hampshire, Massachusetts Bay Rhode-Island, Connecticut, New-York, New-Jersey, Pennsylvania, Delaware, Maryland, Virginia North-Carolina, South-Carolina, and Georgia,* TO

John Paul Jones, Esqure,

WE, reposing especial Trust and Confidence in your Patriotism, Valour, Conduct, and Fidelity, DO, by these Presents, constitute and appoint you to be *Captain* of the armed ———— called the ———— in the Service of the United States of North-America, fitted out for the Defence of American Liberty, and for repelling every hostile Invasion thereof. You are therefore carefully and diligently to discharge the Duty of *Captain* by doing and performing all manner of Things thereunto belonging. And we do strictly charge and require all Officers, Marines and Seamen under your Command, to be obedient to your Orders as *Captain* And you are to observe and follow such Orders and Directions from Time to Time as you shall receive from this or a future Congress of the United States, or Committee of Congress for that Purpose appointed, or Commander in Chief for the Time being of the Navy of the United States, or any other your superior Officer, according to the Rules and Discipline of War, the Usage of the Sea, and the Instructions herewith given you, in Pursuance of the Trust reposed in you. This Commission to continue in Force until revoked by this or a future Congress.

DATED at *Philadelphia October* 10ᵗʰ 1776

By Order of the CONGRESS,

John Hancock   PRESIDENT

This document is John Paul Jones's commission as a captain in the Continental navy. Congress commissioned John Paul Jones in 1776. It is signed by John Hancock.

This illustration shows the USS Alfred in 1775. Captain John Paul Jones commanded the Alfred from 1776 to 1777.

ships sailing between Rhode Island and ports on Long Island Sound. He later captured 16 British ships. He burned eight of them and sent eight into port as prizes. Jones was promoted to the rank of captain and put in command of the larger *Alfred* as reward for his success.

In March 1777, Jones decided to go to Philadelphia to propose a new naval **strategy** to congress. He wanted to capture British ships. If he did so, the American government could get the prize money from the sale of the ships and use the money to win the war.

On June 14, 1777, congress made Jones the captain of the *Ranger*. It was the same day that congress determined what the American flag should look like. The *Ranger* was built for battle. It had 18 cannons and a crew of 140 men.

By late October, the *Ranger* was ready to sail, and on November 1, it put out to sea. Jones's orders were to sail to France and then begin looking for British warships to capture. On the way to France, Jones trained his crew to sail and use the guns. One of his men reported that Jones was "sweet like a vine when he wished, but when necessary, like a rock." The transatlantic crossing took four weeks.

This oil painting shows the Ranger receiving the salute from the French fleet at Quiberon Bay, France, on February 14, 1778. This was the first recognition of the American flag by a foreign government.

INVADING ENGLAND

When Jones arrived in France, he got orders from Benjamin Franklin, Arthur Lee, and Silas Deane that allowed him to do anything in his power to hurt the British. Jones decided not just to attack British trade but also to lead men ashore onto British land. He also planned to capture an important British government official whom he could exchange for captured American sailors.

Jones decided to attack the English town of Whitehaven and the ships in its harbor. Jones set fire to the ship *Thomson*. He then went to St. Mary Isle to kidnap the Earl of Selkirk to exchange for American sailors. The earl sent people to say he was not at home. Jones was tricked and went away.

Instead of returning to France, he crossed the Irish Sea, where he fought with the British ship *Drake*. Jones forced the *Drake* to surrender. He sailed the captured British ship into Brest, the headquarters of the French navy. Jones had become famous on both sides of the Atlantic for his daring, and this boosted the morale of the patriots in America. Jones's success was important because at this time, two ships of the Continental navy had been lost within 90 days.

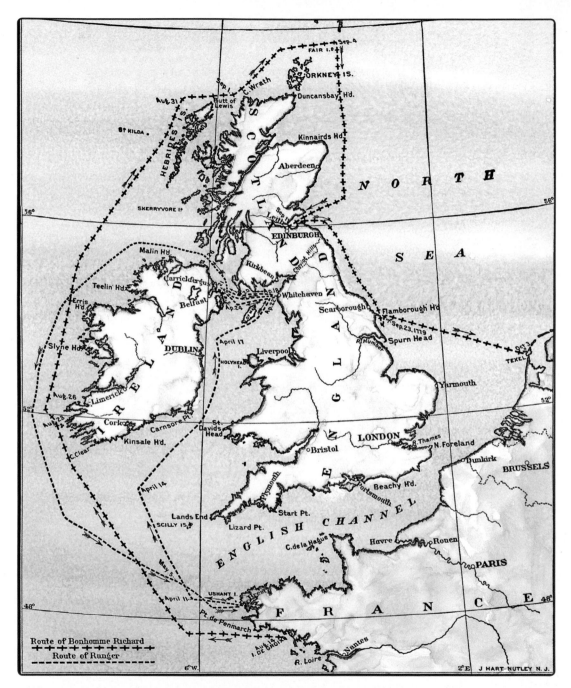

This map shows the routes of the American ships Ranger *and* Bonhomme
Richard *among the British Isles.*

"I HAVE NOT YET BEGUN TO FIGHT"

After the capture of the *Drake*, Jones waited in Paris for a new ship. Writing of his daring, he said, "I wish to have no connection with any Ship that does not sail fast; for I intend to go in harm's way." Because Jones was such a brave sailor, the king of France, an ally of America, gave him a ship. Jones called it the *Bonhomme Richard*. Jones was also given five additional ships to command.

Jones's **squadron** captured six British ships off of northern Scotland. Jones then intended to sail up the River Leith and attack Edinburgh, the capital of Scotland. Bad weather forced him to **abandon** his plan.

On September 23, 1779, Jones's ship engaged the British ship *Serapis* in battle. For three hours, the *Bonhomme Richard* and *Serapis* moved for the best position to fire their cannons. Looking for an advantage, Jones ran the bow of the *Bonhomme Richard* into the stern of the *Serapis*. He ordered his men to tie the boats together. "With my own hands I tied [one of the lines that bound] the *Serapis* to the *Bonhomme Richard*," Jones reported.

This illustration is a dramatic re-creation of the moment when John Paul Jones refused to surrender to the captain of the Serapis. He said at this moment, "I have not yet begun to fight."

The *Bonhomme Richard* and the *Serapis* battled until the pole holding the American flag was shot away. Seeing the heavy damage taken by the *Bonhomme Richard* and seeing that the flag was gone, the British captain, Richard Pearson, shouted out to Jones, asking if he was ready to surrender. John Paul Jones replied, "I have not yet begun to fight." The battle continued until the mainmast of the *Serapis* began to tremble. Seeing that he was beaten, Captain Pearson surrendered.

WINNING THE WAR AND GLORY

When Captain Jones brought the *Serapis* to Holland, he was greeted as a hero. He sailed to France on December 27, 1779, and was honored by King Louis XVI. Jones then set sail for America with many needed supplies for the Continental army and reached Philadelphia in February 1781. Jones was to take command of a new ship, the *America*, being built in New Hampshire.

Jones arrived in Portsmouth at the end of August 1781. On the day of his arrival at Portsmouth, French troops landed in Virginia to help American soldiers force the British to surrender at Yorktown. Three weeks later, General Cornwallis's army surrendered.

With peace won, Jones went to the congress with a plan to expand the American navy, stating that, "In the time of peace, it is necessary to prepare, and be always prepared for war by sea." It is for this reason and his undying dedication to the American cause of liberty that John Paul Jones is considered the father of the American navy. On July 18, 1792, less than a month after his 45th birthday, Jones died in Paris.

GLOSSARY

abandon (uh-BAN-din) To leave and never return to.

apprenticed (uh-PREN-tisd) Attached oneself to a master at some profession in order to learn the business.

epidemics (eh-puh-DEH-mihks) Times when diseases spread very quickly and affect a large number of people.

merchant (MUR-chint) A person who buys, sells, and trades merchandise.

militia (muh-LIH-shuh) A group of people who are not part of the armed forces of a country but are trained like soldiers.

mutinous (MYOO-tuh-nuhs) Feeling or showing a desire not to do what someone has told or ordered you to do.

navigation (nav-i-GAE-shin) The act of finding the way to get to a place when you are traveling in a ship.

Parliament (PAHR-luh-muhnt) The group of people who are responsible for making the laws in Great Britain.

provisions (pruh-VIH-zhunz) A supply of food and other things that are needed.

salary (SAA-luh-ree) An amount of money that an employee is paid each year.

squadron (SKWAH-druhn) A military unit consisting of soldiers, ships, or aircraft.

strategy (STRAA-tuh-jee) A careful plan or method for achieving a goal.

INDEX

PRIMARY SOURCE LIST

Page 5: *Victoria Dock* was created in 1885, artist unknown. The painting is of the dock in Aberdeen Scotland, completed in 1848 and named after Queen Victoria.

Page 7: Map of North America and the West Indies by Carington Bowles, created in 1774.

Page 9: Illustration from *A Compleat History of Druggs*, by Pierre Pomet (1658–1699). He was a doctor to King Louis XIV (1638–1715). Originally published in 1694, France; English-language version in 1725, London.

Page 11: Printed release, witnessed by William Cooper, town clerk of Boston on June 17, 1774. John Adams was moderator.

Page 13: *Battle of Bunker Hill*, created in 1909 by E. Percy Moran (1862–1935). Official photographs of the painting are at the Library of Congress Prints and Photographs Division, Washington, D.C.

Page 14: Image of congressional paper from 1776. It declares the commission of John Paul Jones as Captain in the American Navy.

Page 19: *Courses of the Ranger and Bonhomme Richard on their Cruises about the British Isles*, antique woodcut from *Scribner's Magazine*, published in 1898 by Charles Scribner's Sons, New York.

WEBSITES

Due to the changing nature of Internet links, PowerKids Press has developed an online list of websites related to the subject of this book. This site is updated regularly. Please use this link to access the list: www.powerkidslinks.com/soah/jpj